SUPER
CHARGE
Your Brand

Other Books by Jerrold R. Jenkins

Publish to Win: Smart Strategies to Sell More Books

Inside the Bestsellers

The Independent Publisher:
How to Build and Promote Your Best-Selling Book

Published by
Jenkins Group, Inc.
Traverse City, MI

Publisher's Cataloging-in-Publication Data
Greece, Mike.

  Supercharge your brand : the amazing power of books as marketing tools /
  Mike Greece, Jerrold R. Jenkins, with Rebecca Chown. – Traverse City, MI :
  Jenkins Group, Inc., 2017.

  p. ; cm.

  ISBN13: 978-0-9860224-4-9

  1. Business writing. 2. Marketing. I. Title. II. Jenkins, Jerrold R.
  III. Chown, Rebecca.

HF5718.3.G74 2017
808.06665—dc23   2016961963

FIRST EDITION

Project coordination by Jenkins Group, Inc.
www.JenkinsGroupInc.com
www.BooksAreMarketingTools.com

Design by Yvonne Fetig Roehler

Printed in the United States of America
21   20   19   18   17   •   5   4   3   2   1

SUPER CHARGE
Your Brand

THE AMAZING POWER OF BOOKS AS MARKETING TOOLS

MIKE GREECE
JERROLD R. JENKINS
WITH REBECCA CHOWN

JENKINS GROUP
Traverse City, MI

This book is dedicated to the independent authors who have trusted our counsel and advice over the past two decades to create lasting legacies for their insights, knowledge, and achievements.

Also, special thanks to our talented and accomplished wives Joyce and Julie and to our very special children and grandchildren who are the daily inspiration for our work and the anchors for our lives.

CONTENTS

Foreword

Last year, I was looking for a way to share a message I had developed from my experience working on strategic business development. As a veteran in the field, I had witnessed firsthand the power of partnership across multiple businesses and markets. I knew my insight on the topic would not only be beneficial to entrepreneurs and investors but also would cement my own status as an expert on business development. Positioning my unique message in an effective way would allow me to propel both my personal and corporate brand. But a significant challenge remained: what was the most effective way to share my message?

In the Digital Age, we turn to the internet for everything—business transactions, sharing information, differentiating ourselves and our companies from the competition. In fact, today's internet is essentially the grid for individual and enterprise communications across all seven continents. So it wouldn't be off base to turn to the internet as the natural way to communicate my message, right?

Ironically, it is that very dependency on the internet that made it the wrong place to best share my insight. The cluttered and noisy digital landscape often drowns out the message, desensitizing the intended recipient. As I recognized how difficult it was to stand out above this clatter, the necessity of finding an alternate channel for my message became clear.

The answer was simple: I needed to publish a book. Savvy business leaders have been rediscovering books as brand-building tools and have seen powerful results. The book format would give me the chance to elaborate and hone in on my unique message while setting me apart from the maelstrom of content on the internet.

The execution, however, seemed challenging. The process of writing a book is daunting to many, as is publishing and marketing the final product. Yet with the help of Mike Greece and Jerrold Jenkins, the process became straightforward and doable. Over the past two decades, the two have successfully guided numerous publishing projects, helping individuals like me put together high quality, informative books that elevate a personal or professional brand. Their expertise helped me produce my business management strategy book *The Sumo Advantage: Leveraging Business Development to Team with Heavyweights and Grow in Any Economy*. With their insight, I was able to navigate the unfamiliar waters of publishing while —most importantly—maintaining my own unique vision for the project.

In the following pages, Mike and Jerry present tips and information meant to guide even the biggest publishing novice through the creative process. *Supercharge Your Brand: The Amazing Power of Books as Marketing Tools* draws on their extensive experience to thoroughly demystify the process and provide a road map for getting a book project done with ease.

Additionally, for the benefit of burgeoning thought leaders like me, it focuses on how to use a book to truly cut through the fog of competing ideas. Mike and Jerry have honed in on the best and most effective way to get a message where it needs to be. Beyond just a simple how-to-publish guide, *Supercharge Your Brand* positions the necessary information inside a larger framework relevant to business leaders, allowing readers to fully harness the potential of their book.

— BERNIE BRENNER
Co-founder and Chief Strategy Officer, TrueCar, Inc.
Author, *The Sumo Advantage*
Host, Extreme Biz Dev podcast
www.berniebrenner.com

Introduction

A POWERFUL GAME CHANGER FOR BUSINESSES AND BRANDS

Bill Gates, Steve Jobs, Jack Welch, Sheryl Sandberg, and Lee Iacocca are all icons of corporate leadership and success. What else do they have in common? They've all used a book to differentiate themselves in their respective markets and to push their companies and brands to the forefront, generating new and exciting business opportunities.

The chief benefit of publishing a book is how it magnifies an author's or organization's aura and influence. The return on investment (ROI) that follows—credibility, authenticity, longevity, and legacy—provides the requisite credentials for selling, growing, consulting, teaching, speaking, or whatever business goal is on the table.

Customers, prospects, and consumers know that books reflect authority, trust, expertise, and knowledge. That's why we so seldom throw them away. In today's fast-paced and digital world, those who write a book have an advantage over the competition. In fact, typically the smaller the company, the bigger the impact.

Compare the unfailing simplicity of a thoughtful, well-constructed book with the barrage of e-mails, texts, Twitter feeds, Facebook messages, blog posts, articles, and ads we receive daily. In many organizations, this battery of marketing initiatives gobbles up time and money because it requires endless new stuff to feed the beast.

No wonder so many people cope with the racket by pressing the delete button. Digital marketing is increasingly overwhelming, high maintenance, and perishable.

By contrast, a well-constructed business book has staying power, authority, and respectability. This permanence can maximize marketing success with a top-of-mind brand keepsake that endures. It does this by addressing a problem and delivering actionable insights, education, vision, and prescriptive advice.

Not too many years ago, book lovers and bookstore owners around the world feared that the digital world replete with e-books and e-readers heralded the demise of hardcover books. According to Amazon, not so! As reported in 2016, the number of hard- or softcover books in Amazon's Business and Money category is as follows:

Economics:	913,459
Management and Leadership:	272,413
Marketing/Sales:	94,239
Accounting:	61,749
Process/Infrastructure:	78,935
Skills:	73,916
Small Business/Entrepreneurship:	66,669
Business Culture:	28,070

One reason for the persistence of books as marketing tools is that many shrewd businesses, particularly in the service sector, where technical or product innovation is difficult, have discovered the staying power of the custom-published book. It is the most effective way to send a missile to targeted groups of people to increase the author's or brand's footprint and voice, thus creating desirability as a trusted advisor, business resource, or partner.

Imagine the immediate and long-term effect of a chief executive officer who wrote the book on a subject that helps or invigorates you, your business, or your workforce. Imagine handing a potential client a book rather than a business card and the impression that makes. Inevitably, it validates you as an expert in your field.

By facilitating conversations and influence, books move authors from anonymous to well known. Not surprisingly, well-crafted business books have proven to be transformational for businesses and individuals of all shapes and sizes, leveling the playing field with much larger entities.

Supercharge Your Brand: The Amazing Power of Books as Marketing Tools is a one-stop guide to creating, publishing, and using the business book to enhance your professional, organizational, and personal success. It can catapult you out of obscurity and into category leadership. The following chapters and appendices offer advice for authors who wish to use this timeless, elemental, and immutable marketing tool to supercharge their businesses and their lives.

— MIKE GREECE and JERROLD R. JENKINS

Co-authors Mike Greece and Jerrold R. Jenkins have worked together as content coaches and advisors, public relations and marketing experts, and independent book publishers for more than 25 years. Together, they have helped hundreds of authors across the globe create impactful books that have been successfully used as effective marketing tools.

Chapter 1

"WHY THIS BOOK? WHY NOW?" THE NEED FOR RELEVANCE

How profound that "author" is the root of the word "authority"!

In a noisy and global digital marketplace, increasing sales, influence, brand preference, and particularly mind and market share have become painfully expensive, time consuming, and elusive, particularly in competitive areas such as the service sector, where the lure of shiny new products is impractical. Millions of dollars are spent every year on a plethora of integrated marketing tactics that need constant renewal. Return on investment is also difficult to measure.

Over the past two decades spent helping brands with global and national marketing initiatives at the highest levels, we've seen just how hard chief executive officers (CEOs), chief marketing officers (CMOs), and brand managers work to stimulate sustainable market interest. They call on an endless menu of tactics ranging from media relations to advertising to search engine optimization (SEO), search engine marketing (SEM), word of mouth (WOM), direct mail/e-mail, and most recently the insatiable jukebox of content marketing known as brand journalism.

Through marketing campaign after marketing campaign, we've watched CEOs and brands that achieved modest success attracting market attention suddenly gain rock star status after authoring a book. Over and over, we've watched these books become door openers with prospects and catapult small, midsize, or supersize companies in noisy markets.

In service and advisory firms such as law and consulting, where it's hard to invigorate interest, the fresh thinking codified in a book is key to stimulating interest and acceptance. The same goes for motivational or legacy authors who write books to share lessons they've learned while growing a business or overcoming obstacles.

Invariably, people want to learn from and engage authors. Books spawn recognition leading to top-of-mind awareness, speaking opportunities, workshops, boot camps, and ultimately the allure of thought leadership.

According to the Publishing Institute, a carefully constructed business book boosts revenue 380% for consultants, 219% for public speakers, and 194% for real estate agents. A book can open doors with prospects while reassuring current clients and stakeholders of a brand's validity, authenticity, credibility, and suitability.

The marketing benefits of high-value business books abound. Consider the following list. Business books:

- Brand you as a thought leader who owns the authority
- Create differentiation, reaching targeted groups of people with information relevant to their needs
- Open doors otherwise closed to cold callers, e-mails, and brochures
- Enhance your credibility by permanently showcasing your expertise and vision
- Exert influence, educating and engaging prospects and customers
- Build personal relationships and stimulate word of mouth
- Elevate your authenticity and legitimacy and validate you and your brand
- Generate leads and act as bait for prospecting
- Level the playing field if you're David fighting Goliath
- Serve as a permanent and highly credible leave-behind
- Immortalize your personal legacy and body of work

A caveat: books as marketing tools (BAMTs) usually aren't meant to be *New York Times* best sellers. Instead, they're mostly engines for driving business generation. The key to success is relevancy and giving upfront answers to the questions "Why this book?" and "Why now?"

To accomplish this, authors should create a book that does the following:

- shares a winning model
- offers motivation or inspiration

Once your book is published, it becomes a calling card while your competitors rely on a cornucopia of relentless marketing initiatives and sales tactics.

One useful first question you should ask yourself is what problem you can demystify? What prescription of fresh, helpful thinking can you bring to the table? What stories can you tell that resonate within your target audience?

If you're writing about an issue in the target market, bear in mind that it must be one that keeps many people awake at night. This problem must be real, not imagined or manufactured, and it must affect a broad swath of readers. The greatest business books appeal to their readership because lots of people have this problem, not just one.

For example, international business consultant Mark Brown's recently published book *The Empathic Enterprise: Winning by Staying Human in a Digital Age* focused on a problem everyone understood but had yet to face head on. Mark defined the challenge and allayed the global business community's concerns about properly balancing touch versus tech in a world where most companies now overuse technology.

His book immediately garnered rave reviews from existing clients as well as prospects who asked Mark to assess and help balance their touch/tech scales both internally and externally.

Mark's catchy title helped the book succeed and do what great titles are supposed to do: cause readers to say, "What do you mean by that?" and seek an explanation through engagement with the author. More on that later.

Not every BAMT addresses a problem. Here are other examples of the genre:

- A personal memoir of business success
- A legacy book to commemorate a company milestone or anniversary
- A guidebook to teach a new skill, differentiate the brand, or share a position of the author

Every successful author wants his or her book to add value. The question is, how do they accomplish this?

Consider the following four critical elements:

1. GREAT BUSINESS BOOKS HELP RATHER THAN SELL

First and foremost, great business books are helpful, not self-serving. This is the critical factor in creating market interest, acceptance, and excitement through word of mouth and buzz.

A book's value lies in its inspiration, vision, and data that can be applied to a problem. A tool kit such as this can expand a brand's standing and reputation within a target audience.

This value must be prescriptive, educational, informative, analytical, new, forward looking, and above all worth keeping. It also has to be "you" centered, not "me" centered. As Jay Baer's highly successful book by the same title so aptly illustrates, your book must have "Youtility."

Most people today don't want to be sold. They want information, not propaganda. So craft your book to help them. Clarify, guide, illuminate, motivate, inspire—do all this, and you'll create interest and a successful book.

If your book doesn't offer benefits—if it's little more than a commercial for you or your business—you will likely be disappointed in its use as a marketing vehicle. On the other hand, writing on a subject you are passionate and knowledgeable about that connects to a timely platform or that inspires readers to overcome their own obstacles will magnify your influence, differentiate you, and further your opportunity to do business.

2. GREAT BUSINESS BOOKS ARE SUSTAINABLE

In addition to honing in on an issue that strikes a nerve in readers, great business books achieve long-term sustainability by providing solutions and/or a vision that resonates into the future.

Not only are these books "keepers," but also the fresh perspective or thought leadership they offer is compelling enough that readers want to pass these books on to colleagues, coworkers, and clients. Brand journalism propagated on the web comes and goes, but "Word of Book" (WOB) is permanent.

Dan Prisciotta's book *Defend Your Wealth: Protecting Your Assets in an Increasingly Volatile World* touted the clear danger posed to Americans' individual assets in 2012, particularly the looming threat to personal wealth as global and national economic forces continued to be volatile. The emotional appeal in the title for which Dan presented solutions created an abundance of new prospects for him as well as his Lincoln Financial colleagues across the country.

3. GREAT BUSINESS BOOKS HAVE GREAT TITLES

The ideal title is emotionally driven, memorable, repeatable, and provocative. It usually offers a juxtaposition, oxymoron, alliteration, irony, contradiction, or play on words that causes readers to ask, "What does that mean?" or "Could that help me?" Such a title compels people to open the book and start reading—at first the introduction and most often the first paragraph of the initial chapter. So it is critical for all of these touch points to be convincing that there's value in the coming pages.

A great title also streamlines content development during the writing phase. Think of the backbone of a fish. All the bones—i.e., the ideas and support—join up from the sides connected to the backbone, which provides a unifying theme that the remaining content strengthens.

A brief examination of a few business book titles currently on the shelves confirms the importance of the title in sparking reader interest. Note that each of these head titles is short, three or four words, and that all but one are supported and illuminated by a longer subtitle. Note also the relevance and mass appeal.

- *The Power of the Other: The Startling Effect Other People Have on You, from the Boardroom to the Bedroom and Beyond—and What to Do about It* by Dr. Henry Cloud. By establishing that we are all affected by others but that we aren't powerless, the author positions himself as an expert who can help us with one of our most collectively difficult tasks—dealing with other people.

- *The Perfect Engine: Driving Manufacturing Breakthroughs with the Global Production System* by Anand Sharma and Patricia E. Moody. The word choices in this title are deliberate and irresistible. "Perfect," "Breakthroughs," and the technique called "the Global Production System" appeal to those seeking their own perfection in running a manufacturing enterprise through creating a culture of continuous improvement.

- *Unleash Your Inner Company: Use Passion and Perseverance to Build Your Ideal Business* by John Chisholm. What an invitation for entrepreneurs of all kinds! Who can resist?

- *The World Is Flat: A Brief History of the Twenty-First Century* by Thomas L. Friedman. This title upends our existing belief system. Isn't the world round? What does he mean? And so it begins.

- *The Four-Hour Workweek: Escape 9–5, Live Anywhere, and Join the New Rich* by Timothy Ferriss. Four hours? The new rich? Are you kidding? Tell me more!
- Other titles that stir interest include *Brand Be Nimble*, *How to Win Friends and Influence People*, *The Innovator's Dilemma*, *Purple Cow*, and the list goes on.

In summary, five keys to effective titling are ensuring the title is clever, curious, memorable, relevant, and grab-worthy.

4. GREAT BUSINESS BOOKS ARE READABLE

As mentioned earlier, a book's success is usually made or broken in its title and first page. That's when most readers kick the tires and take a test drive before buying. A boring title or lackluster first paragraph gives them the excuse they need to stop reading. To avoid this, open strong and readable, and maintain interest with lean, direct, powerful writing.

Who Moved My Cheese? by Spencer Johnson and Kenneth Blanchard is one of the most successful business books ever written. Some people say this is because it is so approachable and easy to read.

Avoid multiple-syllable words used simply for the sake of trying to look smart. Create a visual image with words. Instead of "connect," use "build a bridge." Also avoid long case studies and excessively detailed research that can overextend a reader's visit. Tell stories, but keep them short and pithy. Modern readers do not have a long attention span. Use words that have semantic oomph—dollar words, not nickel words. "Good" is a weak word. "Exceptional" is better.

Other land mines include sexist language, inconsistent and passive tenses, a pompous tone, too many long sentences, too many short sentences (for best results, mix them up), and using the pronoun "I." It's tempting to talk about ourselves when sharing solutions, but this perspective seldom belongs in a business book. Readers already know it's you. After all, your name is on the cover. Compare these two sentences:

"I believe consultants should follow these four guidelines …"

versus

"Best practices suggest following four guidelines …"

Not only is it far more interesting to write in the third person, but also "I feel" and "I believe" often alienate readers because these phrases appear to reflect opinion rather than fact. In a business book, authoritative writing that encompasses yet disguises your point of view is far more effective. The exception to this is a company or personal memoir that of necessity includes "I." Even then, don't overdo it.

To guarantee you're on the right track with words worth reading, evaluate your own word skills and then consider engaging the services of a strategic content advisor or coach. As Bill Gates says, "Everyone needs a coach."

If readers sense a lack of professionalism and flow in your writing, your credibility will be destroyed and your BAMT potential squandered.

In the end, incorporating these four critical elements makes your book successful and allows you to fulfill your intrinsic purpose in writing a book: to supercharge your brand or cement your legacy with a permanent, timeless, relevant message via this Holy Grail of marketing tools.

Chapter 2

AN IMPORTANT FIRST STEP: CREATING A STRATEGIC ARCHITECTURE

A well-conceived business book illuminates the landscape.

To get the optimal return on your BAMT, you must think strategically up front, before you begin writing, so that as you develop your outline and chapters, you craft them to a unified end goal and target the appropriate audience so your words (1) have mass appeal and (2) are "media-genic."

In addition to addressing the twin questions discussed in the previous chapter ("Why this book?" and "Why now?"), you should consider the business objective your book will support. Do you want to increase sales, attract speaking engagements, generate leads, expand your consulting, differentiate your brand, grow your business, mobilize readers, compete with the whales, establish yourself as a teacher, speaker, or category authority, or some combination of these?

Further, who is your audience? What problem can you help solve or codify? How will your readers (and you) use the book? Your success lies in figuring out in advance—optimally, before you write a single word—what your objective is, who will read your book, and how they will benefit from it.

At this point, fully aware of your goal, your audience, and the importance of connecting your theme to the issues in your target market, you're ready to design the strategic architecture of your book. One effective blueprint, particularly in a business-to-business (B2B) book, is a simple two-step process that (1) identifies the problem and (2) delivers a solution for alleviating it.

This methodology offers a flight plan for many visionary business books, but depending on your business and your specific goals, other trajectories also work. Take CEO Ralph Braun's inspirational book *Rise Above: How One Man's Search for Mobility Helped the World Get Moving*.

Diagnosed with muscular dystrophy at age six, Ralph eventually began using a wheelchair. As he grew older, he needed to find a way to get to work. *Rise Above* tells his customers and distributors how he outfitted an old postal Jeep with hand controls and a hydraulic lift and how, as his mobility increased, he built an automotive conversion company that created mobility for hundreds of thousands of disabled people. BraunAbility eventually became the largest manufacturer of wheelchair-accessible vehicles in the world.

Rise Above offers a powerful example of a true entrepreneurial spirit, but it doesn't address a specific business-oriented problem. Instead, it creates an inspirational narrative related to Ralph's business that conveys how he refused to let his disability hold him back and how he serves as a role model to create mobility for many others. It highlights the value for people with disabilities (Ralph's target audience) by connecting his personal story to his business's value proposition: building wheelchair-accessible vans and vehicles. BraunAbility placed a copy of the book in every van sold.

Other types of business books that veer away from the classic two-step process include legacy books written to commemorate milestones such as the hundredth anniversary of the Archer Daniels Midland (ADM) company, Harley Davidson, Boeing, Chevrolet, and Goodyear Tires. Guidebooks or primers such as those written to showcase best practices, vision, or thought leadership are another type of impactful BAMT.

Your business, your topic, and your goals will impact how you choose to structure your book. While this can be freeing for authors, it can also cause paralysis if you aren't sure how to begin. Again, as needed, this might be the time to engage a strategic content advisor or coach to help you.

If your book does lend itself to the classic two-part approach, read on for a closer look at the path to success.

STEP 1: A CALL TO ARMS

The opening salvo of the most successful business vision books is either (1) why the book is important to readers or (2) a compelling assessment of a threat and a call to arms that resonates with the audience being targeted, often with data and proof points.

Like a modern-day Paul Revere, authors of such books warn readers about a clear and urgent trend or danger they will help solve.

As discussed in the previous chapter, this means keeping readers' needs in mind by conveying your expertise and intentions without turning your book into a monument to you. It means including content that offers insight and solutions for today *and* tomorrow so that your book stays fresh and sustainable. You are writing this book to help others. Determine what they need to understand and how you are going to convey it so that they find your book useful—perhaps essential. This process will help you structure a two-part outline and determine the appropriate content elements.

Remember business consultant Mark Brown, who wrote *The Empathic Enterprise* to address the modern era's overdependence on technology? Through his consulting work on business performance improvement, Mark observed that the common casualty in an era of increasing reliance on technology was the human connection. After careful analysis, he concluded that in several industries, people wanted more human touch, while in other industries, they wanted less.

This was an "Aha" moment for Mark. His goal was to use actionable insights from his practice to expand his business with existing and prospective clients.

Exposing a highly relevant business problem was indeed an effective mobilization technique. Upon seeing the book and its mysterious title, clients reached out to talk to Mark about their version of the touch-versus-tech conundrum and to seek his prescription for achieving proper balance.

Keep in mind that you must have authority to be credible about the problem you are addressing. Mark's credibility was clear—he was a well-known global business performance consultant—but it isn't always so evident.

CONVEY YOUR AUTHORITY

A more complicated scenario occurred when a renowned oncologist wrote a book on alternative investing and struggled to find a PR firm to help promote it. In light of the thousands of books already available on this topic written by professionals with credentials, this author lacked the authority to write credibly on investing for a general audience.

A content advisor coached the doctor on the improved feasibility of tailoring his investing book for a narrower, more relevant category of potential readers: his fellow medical professionals. After all, many of his colleagues didn't have the time or training to figure out how to invest their money.

This segmenting of his content had huge ramifications. The doctor found that with his knowledge, he could create a sellable book if he refocused on investing insights for his peers rather than for readers at large. Although he'd already written his book, he was inspired to go back and narrow the scope of his audience by writing for his fellow MDs.

STEP 2: ROAD MAP TO THE SOLUTION

The second part of the strategic architecture of the classic problem/solution business book delivers a prescription to the cure. In some books, it's possible to give this step-by-step explanation in a single chapter. In other books, it requires multiple chapters. Either way, the solution makes your book valuable. You are offering a way to solve the problem.

By extension, it's crucial to create a chapter outline upfront that adequately delivers on steps 1 and 2, stating the problem before solving it with thoughtful content. The high-level strategic chapter outline on the next page is from an author whose business offers breakthrough solutions to combat early childhood reading deficits. The first three chapters offer an overview of the issue and the remaining chapters explore a variety of solutions.

HIGH-LEVEL STRATEGIC CHAPTER OUTLINE FOR BOOK ON THE URGENCY OF CLOSING CHILDREN'S EARLY READING GAP

Chapter 1: The Threat

- Why is this book important? Why now?
- Overview of current failed early reading skills: reading gap growing on first day of school; new expectations in kindergarten; growing evidence of consequences to short- and long-term success
- Economic impact and burden on employers, nation
- Data and future implications in an increasingly fierce global economy

Chapter 2: Importance of a Preemptive Rather Than Remedial Strategy

- Describe two significant windows of opportunity:
  (1) preschool years and parental behavior
  (2) kindergarten and grade 1 teacher challenges
- Current landscape failing children
- Urgency of imparting initial reading skills at home
- Need for holistic emphasis and collaborative attention
- The legacy of step-by-step reading, i.e., *Dick and Jane* books (circa 1950s)

Chapter 3: Experts and Studies Confirm the Fail

- Proof points regarding serious nature of problem

- University studies and findings
- Charts and graphs

Chapter 4: The [insert branded process] Way

- Genesis of movement
- What we learned and how it applies
- Sharable methodology, tools, tactics
- Urgency for culture change
- Need for partnership (parents and teachers)

Chapter 5: Early Adopters Find Success—Where the [insert branded process] Way Is Working

- Current exemplars

Chapter 6: Making a Difference, One Reader at a Time

- Mini-cases and testimonials (kids, parents, and teachers)

Chapter 7: What You Can Do

- Parents: Reconnecting with preschool children
- Teachers: Assessment and early attention
- Education leaders (superintendents, principals): leadership and tools

Chapter 8: Vision for the Future: "Reading Is a Team Sport"

- Author's overview, insights, advice
- Takeaways
- Summary and conclusion

Just as there's more than one way to skin a cat, there's more than one way to structure an outline. Assuming your book lends itself to this two-step approach, establish a valid issue and offer clear, actionable solutions to make your BAMT successful.

CHECKLIST
FOR DESIGNING YOUR STRATEGIC ARCHITECTURE

The following checklist may help you sort key strategic content issues *before* you begin writing.

Strategic Issues:

1. Does your content reflect fresh, over-the-horizon thinking that differentiates your brand, connects to a business goal, and sets you apart from the competition?

2. Is the topic tied to a genuine and broad problem in your target market?

3. How will you help rather than sell readers?

4. Will your suggested solution(s) be useful and sustainable?

5. How can you use images or graphics to further enhance your message? These could include photographs, line drawings, charts, graphs, illustrations, quizzes, checklists, and more.

You may decide you need help figuring out how to design the strategic architecture of your book. If so, consider it a good investment. You don't paint your own car, you don't make your own golf clubs, and you don't build your own house. You hire professionals to do this work, and, if needed, you should do the same when building your book.

Thinking it through in advance is vital. Authors who do so inevitably find, as the old saying goes, "Well begun is half done."

Chapter **3**

VIRTUES AND ADVANTAGES OF GOING INDIE: HOW TO GET YOUR BOOK DONE

What a business asset to have "written the book" on the subject!

Once upon a time, independent publishing was considered an act of desperation by those who couldn't sell a traditional publisher. Today, independent publishing is widely respected and the quickest and most economical way to get a book done.

According to Wikipedia, in 2016, 80% of the 304,912 books written in the United States were independently published.

Before delving into the mechanics of writing, designing, and publishing a book, it's worth taking the time to talk about the benefits of going indie.

BENEFITS OF INDEPENDENT PUBLISHING

Authors who independently publish maintain control of the content, design, profits, buyers, and timetable. Most independently published authors can go from idea to final product in six to ten months, depending on a variety of factors.

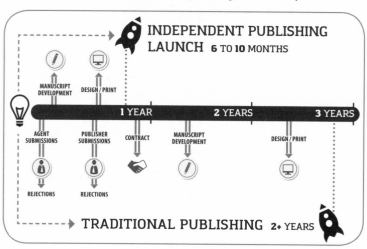

By contrast, those hoping to ink a traditional publishing deal are in for a long slog. The process of pitching a business book to a publisher has become increasingly complex, often requiring the services of an agent to sell the content. Assuming you're successful, it can take a year to get an agent, an additional year to get a publishing deal, and then another one to three years before the book is actually published and launched. Independent publishing eliminates the pitching and approval process that delays getting published.

Beyond that, it's important to note that copyright and book sales questions dominate the decision to publish, typically involving extended periods of time and politicking. As mentioned, thought leadership business books by first-time authors meant to be used as marketing vehicles and targeting a specific audience don't generally carry the mass-market appeal required to make the *New York Times* best sellers list. Consequently, publishers show little interest in these projects.

Independent publishing also delivers a product of the same quality as well as complete editorial and creative control. Authors can decide on the title, the cover art, the content, the interior design, the marketing, the run size (quantity), and of course the length.

Traditionally, larger was seen as better, but these days, independent authors and publishers make their books any length they choose. In today's Twitter-saturated universe, this is the difference between a book that sits on the shelf and one that people actually read. Successful business books are increasingly concise and getting more so, as evidenced during frequent browsing trips to Barnes & Noble. That's just the nature of effective communication today. It's about brevity, about pithiness, about getting it done. This is true for both individual chapters and the overall length of your book.

Today's independent publishing channel distribution options may, in some cases, also reveal exactly who is buying your book, information that authors working with a traditional publisher seldom if ever receive. The benefit of this is clear: authors can directly reach out to and engage those customers who have already exhibited interest in what they have to say.

Finally, independently publishing a book is cost effective. That said, no two books cost the same to publish, nor is it possible to offer up a general dollar figure. The goals and scope of each project are different. One author may want to print 1,000 books while another prints 10,000. Likewise, a marketing budget of $3,000 for the whole project is a lot different than hiring a PR firm with a $3,000 per month retainer.

Keep in mind that the value of the book as a marketing tool isn't the number of books sold but the marketing ability the book provides. As highly successful business owner and entrepreneur Jennifer Kushell, founder and CEO of Your Success Now, said, "My book, *Secrets of the Young & Successful*, changed my life."

Another view on the value of the ROI of publishing a business book comes from Jesse Theodore, content marketing manager at Cylance in Irvine, California: "Books are the ultimate content pillar."

According to R.R. Bowker, more than 1,700 independently published books per day were produced in 2015. In the end, the vast majority of authors find it pays to independently publish their thinking and body of knowledge. As one business author said, "One new client pays for the entire project."

As the production process moves along, you'll need to pay for editorial and design services and also market your own book, accepting the fact that these investments of time and money are part of the business of writing and publishing a book to enhance your brand.

That said, let's take a closer look at what it takes to write a book and, in so doing, erase a pervasive myth.

IT'S NOT THAT HARD!

The process of writing a book is pretty straightforward, so it's important to address the widespread myth that crafting a book is too hard, too daunting. These objections are solvable. What's more, writing a book will create business growth by supercharging a brand and business.

With apologies to those who experience vertigo at the prospect of writing a book, the actual writing has almost become the easy part of any book project. Regardless of their background or comfort level with writing, astute authors— with the proper support and orientation—can embrace the comprehensive process of outlining, writing, revising, editing, and proofing so that they end up with a compelling and well-written book. Or they can hire a ghostwriter!

Many authors find that the content is waiting inside of them and that it's simply a matter of getting it down on paper. Some people do it themselves while others hire a strategic content advisor or a ghostwriter.

In our experience, the most successful BAMTs do engage a content advisor or marketing expert at the start of the creative process to help outline the ingredients, point of view, and content up front to make the book attractive to media as well as the target audience. These individuals can be invaluable as they help authors create a master plan that determines where to put all the various pieces and parts, much like assembling a new plane or car according to a blueprint.

Depending on your needs and the time and financial resources at your disposal, you may decide to meet with an advisor who can help define the concept of your book and determine its basic structure, essential elements, and a time line that details who is going to do what and by when.

Or, like an increasing number of successful BAMT authors, you may hire a ghostwriter to assemble some or all of the content. Having collectively published more than a thousand books in the past several decades, we've observed that in many of these journeys, a ghostwriter got it done, allowing the author to continue to run his or her business.

Every project is unique; each author's experience is different. Yet in the end, it's all about creating and aggregating an effective team to channel your thoughts into compelling content, then putting it all together in an impactful way.

THE WRITING PROCESS

With or without outside help from content advisors, writing coaches, or ghostwriters, the typical editorial process goes like this:

- Concept development (creating the strategic architecture)
- Creating a working title and chapter outline that guide the flow

- Writing the chapters and integrating data and other research/case studies
- Content editing to enhance or create a powerful opening, middle, and close as well as a compelling final title
- Copyediting or line editing
- Proofreading (your book isn't done once the proofreading is complete, but the remaining steps are encompassed in the design and publishing phases discussed below)

Most of the bulleted items above are self-explanatory, but a few definitions are in order. A working title holds your place, so to speak, while you get started on the writing.

Content editing brings in the big guns—a professional editor who will evaluate your manuscript and point out inconsistencies, organizational problems, or areas that need development. Content editors essentially flesh out what's missing, make sure the existing content is organized and well presented, place artwork, create front and back material, and clarify ambiguous, redundant, or boring writing.

A busy CEO may sometimes turn to a content editor when he or she lacks sufficient time to do the writing. This editor has enough expertise to fill in the blanks and do any research or fact checking that's needed and can also pull information out of the CEO as required. If this sounds a bit like ghostwriting, that's because there's definitely some crossover between ghostwriters and content editors. In fact, they are often one and the same. Both help the author craft the writing needed to create an optimally effective manuscript, but the degree to which they do this depends on the author and the needs of the book.

Copyediting or line editing is for manuscripts that are structurally sound but need to be checked for proper grammar, usage, flow, clarity of writing, spelling, punctuation, and capitalization. A copyedit may also include editing chapter heads, the introduction, the foreword, the preface, the appendices, and the index, if one is included.

Note: content editors sometimes incorporate line editing into their work, but this varies depending on the project, the author, the editor, and the degree of effort that's needed to bring a manuscript to its full potential.

Finally, proofreading involves a final reading of the text to make sure no errors have been missed or have crept into the manuscript during the editing stages. These include errors in grammar, spelling, punctuation, and capitalization as well as style issues and concerns that vary based on the topic and audience for the book.

The number of drafts required to get from concept to the final version of a manuscript will depend upon many factors, all of which can be managed and streamlined by a professional book production company.

Bear in mind that even authors who know exactly what they mean to say don't always convey it clearly on the page, much less catch basic mistakes. This is because writers are too close to their material to be objective. That's where a professional editor is indispensible, but make no mistake: proofreaders are just as important.

When prolific author Guy Kawasaki turned in what he thought was the final copy of one of his independently published books, he was certain it contained no mistakes. To his surprise, the proofreader found 1,400 errors! Had the book gone to press with these errors, Kawasaki's credibility would have been shot.

Above all, don't make the mistake of thinking your aunt, your colleague's spouse, or your college roommate who majored in English can effectively edit your book. That degree might hint at aptitude, but it doesn't guarantee thoroughness or quality. A professional editor will know there is an editing standard to be followed in the book industry, and this differs from the standard followed in the newspaper industry. Newspapers follow the style guide of the Associated Press, while the book industry follows the *Chicago Manual of Style*. The differences between the style guides are at times minute, but it becomes obvious to people in the book industry that your book wasn't professionally edited if it follows the wrong one. You need a working professional to clarify muddy waters when making tricky editorial decisions.

With this cautionary tale out of the way, a few practical and tactical issues to consider as part of the writing and revising process include the following.

Practical Issues to Consider:

1. Who is going to develop the content and write the book? If you've tapped someone to help you and/or have put together a full-fledged book-building team, be sure to collaborate regularly and set clear expectations.

2. Is the time line clear? Is it based on how time sensitive your project is and your own schedule?

3. Can you stay organized so that you expedite the creation and/or delivery of the materials that are to be included in the book instead of slowing the process and derailing the project?

Tactical Issues to Review:

1. Does your book help readers rather than sell them?

2. Is your title memorable and possibly disruptive? Does it serve as the backbone of your book? Do all the main fish bones in your outline come back to this central line?

3. Does your opening sentence/section grab people's attention with a megaphone that trumpets, "The British are coming!"? The first sentence of Dan Prisciotta's book *Defend Your Wealth* reads, "Today, the wealthy in America are under attack." His book is now in its third printing and being used as a marketing tool by the thousands of advisors at Lincoln Financial.

    The second sentence of Richard Shapiro's book *The Endangered Customer* reads, "At no point in our history has your customer base been more vulnerable to poaching than it is today." What business owner or leader wouldn't want to read this book and engage the author?

4. Does the introduction or first chapter explain why this book needs to be read now?

5. Do the point of view and tone of the manuscript empathize with and benefit readers while sustaining a market-centric

focus that creates a sense of urgency and prescribes an antidote?

6. Is the content written primarily in the third person rather than the first person? Does the book focus on your vision and thinking rather than your personal journey? (To repeat, for the most part, avoid "I" and "me.")

7. Does the content align with your experience, business acumen, and service offerings?

8. Will you include an author photo and dedication?

9. Have you solicited a prominent or influential thought leader to provide a foreword for your book?

10. Have you reinforced your book with testimonials, graphics, endorsements, and advanced reviews as discussed below?

11. Does your book add value? Is it a keeper worthy of being passed along?

Reinforcements

Reinforcements just make sense, whether you're building a house, fighting a war, or publishing a book. Reinforcing your book before it goes to print with diverse testimonials, jacket endorsements, and advanced reviews further establishes your credibility. In turn, this makes it more likely that your book will reach its full potential and achieve the goal of positioning you as a trusted authority in your field.

Testimonials and Endorsements. Testimonials and endorsements help transform browsers into buyers. There's a difference between the two: testimonials come from readers, clients, colleagues, and ordinary citizens, and endorsements tend to come from celebrities, industry insiders and gurus, and other big-name authors—from people whose names are known and carry gravitas.

Testimonials don't pack the same punch as celebrity endorsements, but they are essential to your book's overall marketing plan and success. For example, books that include even a single well-written testimonial from a qualified individual stand out and convey professionalism. Books that include many great testimonials stand out even more.

Testimonials and endorsements can be used in a number of places, including the back cover, the inside jacket, the first few pages, and so on. Placement decisions will depend on a number of factors, including their number, their strength, their authority/celebrity, how well they further your specific goals.

Whom will you approach to write a testimonial or endorsement? Seek out people inside and outside your circle of influence who have greater name recognition and a larger following than you, particularly in the space of your target audience. If you're writing a book on finance, an endorsement from Warren Buffett, Suze Orman, or someone of high stature is far more impressive than your next-door neighbor. Credentials matter, so think this through and approach these individuals carefully. If you don't know them personally, you might reach out to their executive assistants with a note and a prepublication galley copy of your book, inviting them to read it and asking whether they'd consider endorsing it.

Use your contacts to target other appropriate individuals you can approach in the same way.

Getting these sought-after words can add time to your project because you may need to halt production to wait for their arrival. However, nearly all authors say these are valuable words worth waiting for.

Advanced Reviews and Published Excerpts. Positive advanced reviews can also reinforce your book. Use galley copies to secure an advanced book review (and potential future jacket endorsement) from potential early adopters and advocates. In addition, if you want to get your book into bookstores, you might need to seek out and pay for an independent review or reviews. Simultaneously, work to get a key chapter or specific excerpt published in an influencer print publication or trade journal.

Writing is creative, but it's also a process. Embrace the process, begin with the end in mind, use time-tested strategies that work, and seek the help you need along the way. Keep in mind that correctly developing your manuscript doesn't necessarily mean changing what you have to say but rather how you say it so that the end result is clear and powerful and above all advances your goals. Remember the fishbone.

THE DESIGN PROCESS

Once your book is written and edited, it's time to hire an experienced book production company to design the interior and exterior. In its entirety, this process encompasses cover and jacket art and design, page layout and text design, proofreading of the layout, and other key elements all geared toward creating just the right look by incorporating new ideas with traditional formulas of success.

Please don't pinch pennies at this stage of the game, because the way your book looks says a great deal about you and your message. The fact is, if you've sufficiently enticed someone to pick up your book, this individual is going to open it and leaf through a page or two. Assuming the inside is as appealing and professional looking as the outside and is accompanied by great writing, you've got 'em.

Skeptical? The following example exhibits how front cover design can send critical subconscious messages about content.

The cover on the left used a three-color palette with flat text on the front and back covers. The professional redesign on the right used richer colors and a sophisticated font. This obliterated the unwritten message of "Schlock consultant publishes book on the cheap!" and replaced it with a professional impression that gave potential customers the confidence they needed to take the next step and give the author a chance.

To paraphrase an old cliché that continues to ring true, people *do* judge a book by its cover. If you can't afford to hire a professional designer for your book, you can't afford to publish. It's that simple. If you're still skeptical, take a look at the following questions and honestly assess your own knowledge.

Do you know the difference between serif and sans serif? Do you know what kerning is? Do you know that different typefaces have different visual sizes? Do you know what a descender is? Or x-height? Or a word block? Or a widow or an orphan? Besides all that, do you want to produce a standard trade paperback or a hardcover book with a dust jacket, embossed cover, gold foiling, and four-color photos? Also, what kind of paper will you use? Do you understand the technical specifications of paper? What are opacity, brightness, and weight? Will the ink bleed through?

All of these elements must be considered when designing your book. Novices can do it, but they won't do it well, and knowledgeable readers will instantly be turned off.

At the same time, keep in mind that hiring a professional to design your book doesn't mean you lose control of the process. The design possibilities may be endless, but you get to provide strategic input and make the final decisions.

The prepress design phase is also the time when you register your book. This means applying for your International Standard Book Number, Library of Congress Card Catalog Number, Publisher's Cataloging in Publication Data, Advance Book Information, barcode, and copyright. Yes, you can do this work yourself, but it's technical and time consuming. You need all the proper registrations if your book is going to be taken seriously. Take the time to do this properly or hire a book production company to help you.

THE PUBLISHING PROCESS

With your manuscript written, edited, proofed, and designed, it's time to publish this new baby you've worked so hard to create. An important tip: try to publish in the first quarter of the coming year so that your book can be touted as new for nine months or more.

PRINTING

Although the creative process is complete, many authors find that sending their book to press spawns as much anxiety as relief. What if they've overlooked critical content? What if lingering mistakes appear in the text? What if no one wants to read it? And how many books should they print anyway?

For books that are being used as marketing tools, the best practice today is to closely examine your audience and marketing goals and print the number of books you need. For example, Orangetheory Fitness printed 100,000 books and sent cases of books to each of its franchises as giveaways to prospective members. On the other side of the spectrum,

Scott Squillace printed 2,000 copies of *Whether to Wed* to boost the standing and notoriety of his law practice. The number of books that works for one person or company won't work for another, but this is part of the beauty of creating a book as a marketing tool. Decisions can be customized to meet your particular needs.

As desired, packaging can also be simple or customized. From printed wraps to custom cardboard sleeves, your book can reach national or international audiences with the look and impression you want.

DISTRIBUTION

Once your books are printed, readily available help in the form of a fulfillment service can deliver them to the destination of your choice, ready for sale, distribution, or both.

Amazon is an easy way for indie authors to sell books online. The downside is that this Internet giant swallows a percentage of the retail price. They also will not provide tracking information about your buyers. This is valuable information that could enhance your marketing database. You can bridge these two worlds by selling your book on your website with both an Amazon link and your own once you establish a fulfillment partner. To track buyers as leads, upgrade your website to highlight your new book and consider direct sales from the site in addition to Amazon.

But wait! Where exactly *do* you want your book to go? What do you do with it once it's published, and how do you get it into the hands of those you wrote it for? That's what the next chapter is all about.

Chapter **4**

DEPLOYING YOUR BOOK: LAUNCHING, LEVERAGING IN THE MODERN MARKETING MIX

A smart business book is a substantial, touchable argument to do business.

A well-written business book is a dynamic vehicle for marketing, which makes the launch of the book big news and fodder that can be used in many different ways.

With a tailored marketing push, your book can create market presence, resulting in an immediate message to readers that you are an undisputed expert in your field. The buzz that's generated will create leads that in turn generate new business.

That said, marketing is a twofold activity. There is marketing the book, i.e., launching it, and there is using the book *for* promotion by integrating it into your marketing mix. This chapter looks at these interrelated activities in terms of three phases: prepublishing, publishing (the launch), and post-publishing.

PREPUBLISHING

Deploying your book requires building a marketing platform in advance. Independent publishing is not a serial process whereby you can write a book today and worry about marketing it tomorrow. If you intend to successfully launch your book and use it as a key part of promoting your business, you need to think about marketing it as soon as you start writing.

The following graphic illustrates the necessary steps, elements, and chronology involved in producing a book.

OVERVIEW OF PROJECT

Authors should evaluate their marketing activities and align them with their business goals for the book before it's published.

For example, a management consultant in Fairfield, Connecticut, may wish to do business in a two- to three-hour radius from the office rather than all over the country. Marketing efforts in this case will be geographically limited, just as business authors based in Europe may wish to market

Savy authors can also do one more thing to establish their credibility: develop an assessment, IQ test, or evaluation matrix. This acts as a call to action and becomes a growth mechanism tool.

Mark Brown of *The Empathic Enterprise* created such a lead-generating marketing tool to engage prospects. This conversation starter consisted of an assessment grid that measured how empathic an enterprise was in meeting the unique tech-versus-touch needs of its customers and other stakeholders.

Giving clients a reason to have a discussion actualizes the promise of the book. It allows clients/potential clients to get a taste of the author and business in a nonthreatening way, without making any promises. To that end, sometimes these assessments are best served complimentarily, as a courtesy, as opposed to more formal interactions or financial commitments that can come later. From agility to performance, virtually anything that can be measured or improved against a pain point in the workplace is fair game. This methodology can serve as a bridge to begin the marketing funnel. This leads to longer-term services in the form of sales, education, training, software, or whatever the author's business happens to be.

PUBLISHING (THE LAUNCH)

Once the book is published, a whole host of marketing opportunities present themselves. These include simple things such as issuing a press release announcing the arrival of the book in finite traditional and social media. Other options are to post a review of the book on Amazon and to send signed copies along with a personal note to a limited cadre of influential clients and significant past clients to get their feedback, make them feel special, and give them the information needed to spread word of mouth. If a book encompasses training, authors may wish to offer boot camps, seminars, or webinars for high-potential prospects who use the book.

Above all, authors must hone in on ways to deliver value out of and make connections via the book's content. They must use the launch of the book as a catalyst for creating conversations and engagement for their brand with clients, prospects, and colleagues.

For example, a few years back, the TBM Consulting Group based in North Carolina was an obscure but trending advisory firm that taught manufacturers the culture and methods of the Toyota Production System. CEO Anand Sharma and his team were relatively unknown in the general business community but getting rave reviews from clients whose businesses they'd transformed by dramatically increasing their profitability. In cases such as Maytag and Pella, TBM's lean teachings were quietly catapulting each brand to category leadership.

To expand, TBM needed to step out from under the shadow of Toyota and own the identity, capacity, and brand recognition to deploy the dogma of lean manufacturing on its own. The solution was one of the best all-time examples of a BAMT. The book written by Sharma with the help of a ghostwriter was used to project his firm's expertise and ability to embed lean into a wide array of manufacturers in different product sectors.

The Perfect Engine: How to Win in the New Demand Economy by Building to Order with Fewer Resources reflected the organic continuous improvement and energy generated in enterprises borrowing from the Toyota Way. The book had broad appeal addressing an achievable goal—a better way to manufacture—but it was how TBM leveraged the book that grew the company's business.

Creating a miniature assembly line model that could be set up on tables in a hotel meeting room, TBM launched a two-day seminar where those engaged in manufacturing—everyone from CEOs to assembly line workers and HR people—could experience the process of making widgets before and after a crash course in TBM's lean training. This allowed everyone to see the difference that lean made in the process. The book was distributed to guide the transformation of the production process, and the seminar itself was branded "Quest for the Perfect Engine."

Demand for the event was high and seats continuously filled on four continents for the next several years. More importantly, a significant number of long-term client engagements accrued from these tastings. Ultimately, market awareness of the transformative powers of TBM's version of the Toyota Way caused businesses to move toward TBM as the trusted agent for the training. As a result of this and other marketing initiatives, TBM's business grew tenfold.

A few years later, Sharma decided to revitalize his brand by writing a second book. This one used the effective technique of reacting to another business author. The book he responded to was *The New Business Normal* by former CEO and business pundit Michael W. Wright. The book showcased the difficulties business leaders were facing. It highlighted the uncontrollable social, economic, and political factors that created a volatile global business environment.

Guess what? Sharna used his brand value proposition and the Toyota Production System—what he already claimed authority and expertise around—as the main tenets of the antidote to global business uncertainty. The new book became a fresh marketing tool for the business.

Because every business is unique, authors have to weigh all their options to deploy their BAMTs successfully. This requires smart targeting and lean marketing to pinpoint tools that will work for their particular book and target audience.

The following is a menu of possible options:

Book Marketing Tactics and Techniques

- Showcase your book at existing or your own relevant workshops, conventions, business meetings, webinars, and seminars

- Create a subject-centric or title-related website to promote it as a destination for sustainable dialogue

- Use social media resources such as Facebook, LinkedIn, Twitter, webcasts, and search engine marketing to create and build an online presence, sustainable community, and following

- Connect with distributors, wholesalers, national bookstore chains, and fulfillment houses to help sell the book

- Submit your book to prepublication and post-publication reviewers to get it noticed

- Add authorship of the book to your résumé, bio, business card, and e-mail signature

- Promote your book via traditional media such as press releases and bylined articles to targeted media such as radio talk shows and business TV

- Investigate multi-city launch events with chambers of commerce and other business organizations

- Blog about your book and reach out to other bloggers who can promote it

- Use the book as an incentive for securing speaking engagements

- List your book with major online retailers

- Sell your book via book clubs, catalogs, and corporations as well as at book shows, trade shows, and national and international exhibits

- Promote your book on Goodreads, the world's largest online portal for readers and book recommendations

- Embrace e-book and enter the digital book market

- Develop promotional materials specifically for your book such as postcards, bookmarks, and posters

- Advertise in trade magazines, depending on your business/approach
- Design a video or visual teaser that can be sent electronically to prospects, encouraging them to buy the book, that includes a replica of the cover, a chapter outline with one or two pithy lines or quotes, a few jacket endorsements, a photo, a bio, sales info, and perhaps a free assessment consultation offer
- Create an audiobook

Hometown bookstores are usually willing to give local authors space, but beyond this, getting your book in a national bookstore is typically Hamburger Hill—in other words, a challenge.

Your energy level, financial resources, and time commitment are the only limiting factors in getting the word out about your book. You can do much of this work yourself, or you can hire professionals to do it. Please be clear on one point: the most successful independent publishers are entrepreneurs who embrace the role of marketing and business expert. They want to change the world in some way, first by writing a book and then by using that book as a marketing tool.

POST-PUBLISHING

Books aren't just a marketing piece. They are a marketing *tool* that can supercharge your brand or business. Because they establish authors as thought leaders and legitimize them as experts, they enrich the prospects for the authors' continued success in ways that social media can't do.

If you are in business, using a book to illustrate and extoll your company's vision is advantageous. If you are a chef, authoring a cookbook confers expert status. If you are a dermatologist writing a book about the threat of sun damage to skin, it will reinforce the prospect of patient engagement. With your new book in hand, you can integrate it into the marketing portfolio of things you are already doing plus embrace new tactics and techniques.

If handled well, your BAMT can mobilize your entire enterprise. Rally your community of mentors, colleagues, and prospects to create conversations about your book. This can be done using simple word of mouth or more complex social media strategies.

Once your book is on the ground, you can also continue to seek presentation and speaking opportunities with influencer groups. These experts can exchange views and highlight your solution.

Richard Shapiro, founder of The Center For Client Retention and author of *The Endangered Customer: Eight Steps to Guarantee Repeat Business*, implemented a variety of techniques to market his newly released book. A leading authority in the area of customer satisfaction and loyalty, he used his book as a calling card to facilitate meetings and speaking opportunities with multiple organizations. The title/topic literally sold itself, as companies and corporations have a keen interest in guaranteeing repeat business. It also contained an emotional appeal in its comparison of the fickle consumer to endangered prey.

Richard gave copies of his book to existing and prospective clients and updated his website to highlight his expertise and authority as a book author. In addition, he created a short video (less than two minutes) featuring excerpts from an interview on Fox News and a book signing that he linked to his website and sent to media and prospective clients.

Like Richard, the more orbits you can penetrate that house potential early adopters, clients, prospective clients, influencers, and even friends and family, the more buzz and leads your book will generate. The secret is to mobilize all these connectors and put them to work for you throughout this exciting period of integrating your book into your marketing mix.

Chapter **5**

EXEMPLARS OF SUCCESS: BOOKS THAT MOVED THE NEEDLE

A book is a tangible and tactile body of proof of expertise, legitimacy, knowledge, and achievement.

What are your goals? Do you want to launch your book to break into a tight market? Are you using it to transition to a new career? Or, are you using your book to provide a solution to a pervasive problem in the business ecosystem? Whatever your goals, this lightning rod called the business book can supercharge your brand, product, or service in the battle for market awareness and traction.

For example, Sarah Susanka was just another architect until she codified her design experience in a 1998 book extolling the virtues of smaller homes. Back then, smaller wasn't better. This was the age of the McMansion. *The Not So Big House* became a best seller, spawning a series of sequels. Now Susanka is a major player in architecture. She's been featured in numerous articles in newspapers, magazines, and online publications. She has appeared on dozens of TV outlets from HGTV to *This Old House* and is much in demand as a speaker in a field she basically created. All because she wrote a book.

What follows is an analysis of six superchargers. None of these books made the *New York Times* best sellers list. Their success was measured in different ways. By enhancing author credibility, building business, offering brand differentiation, and garnering media attention and audience interest, these authors achieved game-changing outcomes.

1

Defend Your Wealth:
Protecting Your Assets in an Increasingly Volatile World
by Daniel A. Prisciotta

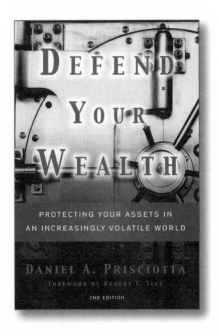

Dan Prisciotta was one of thousands of financial advisors who specialized in helping high-net-worth individuals. He knew he needed something to differentiate himself and attract new clients. He decided to write a book to help people understand how to better manage their assets.

Initially, Dan's working title was *A Guide for High-Net-Worth Individuals*. After zeroing in on his essential message—that people are increasingly vulnerable to losing their assets—he took a harder line. Collaborating with his book marketing team, he transformed his title into three short, powerful words and used the subtitle to convey a sense of urgency. The result was *Defend Your Wealth: Protecting Your Assets in an Increasingly Volatile World.*

This title change supercharged Dan's brand. It became the centerpiece of his marketing efforts, creating the foundation for seminars and professional continuing education credits for other advisors. It also became the main sales tool for most of the financial advisors in Dan's parent company, Lincoln Financial.

The book opened with a threat assessment, highlighting the dangers of those working to protect the assets of individual investors from outside forces. This set Dan and his brand apart from *all* his competitors and became the key to getting face time with clients and new prospects.

Branding Dan as an expert served as a tool for generating credibility, urgency, and authority. It tripled attendance at his seminars. As if that weren't enough, the book catapulted him into the role of prestige advisor at Sagemark Private Wealth Services Group. He also founded and now manages Equity Strategies Group.

2

The Wine Region of Rioja
by Ana Fabiano

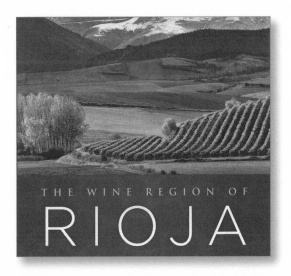

Ana Fabiano's award-winning book *The Wine Region of Rioja* is the most comprehensive book on the Spanish region and its wines. This beautifully illustrated full-color volume pays tribute to Riojan wine making and cuture. It is the only wine book by a United States publisher to be endorsed by the government of Rioja.

Ana is the North American trade director and brand ambasador for Rioja. She wrote the book as a labor of love manifesting her passion, voice, and experience. As a late baby boomer, she was greatly impacted as a young student living in Spain during its transition to democracy; her attachment to the region underlies the book's authenticity.

The Wine Region of Rioja is a legacy book, a collector's item that appeals equally to growers, vintners, distributors, retail establishments, and consumers. Inevitably, its cascading effect offers world-class brand extension for the Riojan region because, beyond a brochure, it provides linkage down the supply chain in competitive product lines.

In her travels, Ana's clients tell her that they enjoy the lush photography and consider the book an object of value in their homes. She explains, "As someone heavily involved in international business and digital technology in multiple time zones, I like to disconnect at some point every day. A book is an ideal way to do this."

Ana published *The Wine Region of Rioja* in 2012. Since then, her work for Rioja has deepened, and her responsibility, territory, and success have grown. Not surprisingly, the book has become a noted source of education and promotion. For example, in her outreach work around North America, Ana often uses the book as an incentive or reward. On a recent trip to Canada, her team partnered with a restaurant to put on a private event. They gave five copies of the book to the restaurant to use as it liked, and in turn the restaurant gave a copy to the first five people who signed up to attend the event.

When the winners were announced, they came up for Ana's autograph. Ana explains that she was unprepared for how meaningful this experience would be. One man asked her to sign the book for his wife so that he could give it to her on their tenth anniversary trip to Rioja.

Now, Ana is planning a second edition of *The Wine Region of Rioja*. The book is more than a reference or historical piece. It must be updated because its subject matter, like wine itself, is dynamic and changing.

Just as the subject matter changes, so do the marketing needs of the book. Promoting it is something Ana does constantly. She comments, "Marketing is a continual dialogue and extension of the work. You can never be static. You always have to be evolving and present."

She concludes, "My book extends Rioja's brand, but it also extends my personal brand. It's the voice of my journey within the region." She adds, "I hope at some point to write entertaining historical fiction that takes my brand beyond *The Wine Region of Rioja* yet continues to highlight this amazing region."

3

The Endangered Customer:
Eight Steps to Guarantee Repeat Business
by Richard R. Shapiro

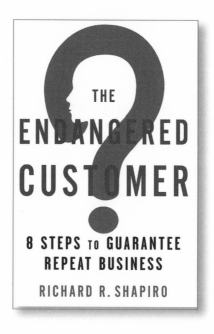

The Endangered Customer: Eight Steps to Guarantee Repeat Business offers a classic example of how books can evolve to convey broad insights on consumer behavior to supercharge the author's brand. As mentioned in the previous chapter, Richard is a leading authority in the area of customer loyalty.

For almost 30 years, he's spearheaded research on companies seeking insights on customer loyalty and repeat business. He wrote his first book, *The Welcomer Edge: Unlocking the Secrets to Repeat Business*, in 2012.

When he decided to write a follow-up book, he focused on the timely conundrum of waning consumer brand loyalty caused by internet shopping. That message, the urgent need to retain customers, along with an eight-step plan, became his brand.

The value was clear—Richard's first book solved the enormous problem of how to keep customers coming back in a digital marketplace. The prescription was easy for businesses of all kinds to implement, thanks to the Repeat Business Scorecard assessment tool he included at the end of the book. *The Endangered Customer* became a runaway success.

The cover was of primary importance. Richard first had to convince people to pick up the book. He hired a professional book designer who created stark visuals to contrast with the provocative title.

Within six months of being published, *The Endangered Customer* opened doors to many lucrative workshops and speaking opportunities. By the end of the year, Richard doubled his billable consulting hours from the prior year. As he happily put it, "My book was a catalyst to open new doors, and I'm enjoying the journey."

Richard noted that working with a content coach drastically improved the material in the book. He commented, "I think authors become immersed in their ideas, concepts, and thoughts and sometimes don't recognize their possible impact."

He added, "After being in busines for 28 years, the book solidified our modalities. The change for our company is that now all research, training, discussions, and consulting lead back to the eight steps."

In hindsight, the evolution of Richard's book may seem obvious and even inevitable, and that's the point: Richard made it look easy, but he put the work in up front to clarify his thinking and his approach, and the product continues to speak for itself.

4

Leadership Rigor:
Breakthrough Performance and Productivity
Leading Yourself • Teams • Organization
by Erica Peitler

Erica Peitler already knew that writing a book would give her an edge. Her first book, *Open Up and Say Ahhh!,* was published in the early days of her consulting company Erica Peitler & Associates. Her goal was to establish herself as a thought leader to both new clients and prior colleagues. The book was a tool to get her material on radio shows.

Her second book, *Leadership Rigor*, represented a way for her to create a deeper relationship with existing clients who were already working with her material. It also responded to the urgent need highlighted in the latest Global Human Capital Trends report published by Deloitte University Press: that one of the most critical needs for companies is building leadership capability. Subsequently, the book became mandatory reading for those interested in achieving breakthrough performance and productivity.

Erica notes that the key to making a book an effective marketing tool is knowing your target audience. You must focus your efforts there while minimizing the temptation to take a "peanut butter spread" approach.

She explains, "My partner often tells me, 'You are looking for the people who are looking for you,' and with marketing a book, this is totally true!" She elaborates, "My first book was for individuals going through personal transitions looking to get unstuck and back on a path of change and growth. My second book was about change and growth from a structured team/organizational perspective. The first one grew my individual coaching practice when I was first starting my business. The second captured the work I had developed during my team/organizational facilitation work. The go-to-market approach was different for each, but both are part of the marketing mix that adds an additional sense of credibility to the work I do."

These consistent and strong reinforcements of Erica's personal brand are a true differentiator. In addition to the experience her podcasts, articles, blogs, websites, and videos offer clients, her books are something people can see, feel, and touch. Erica concludes, "A book is the new tangible 'business card' today."

5

The Empathic Enterprise:
Winning by Staying Human in a Digital Age
by Mark A. Brown

Before he wrote *The Empathic Enterprise*, Mark Brown was one of many independent consultants helping firms and individuals improve their business performance through leadership development training. Often, the material he used was someone else's intellectual property. In reflecting on the process of becoming a first-time business book author, he notes how critical it was for him to offer his own fresh thinking before he began writing.

He recalls, "My coach was very candid with me. He looked over my original idea and said, 'You can do better.' After we looked at the competition, I realized there were thousands of books out there on the very general topic of how to improve your business performance. I wanted to create my own intellectual property. I had the knowledge to write about a strategy that was broadly relevant and timely. This set me on a different path."

Mark's insightful book addressed the increasing overreliance by many companies on technology and the need for balance between tech and touch. This idea to improve the customer experience created opportunities for Mark to revisit clients with his new insights.

Mark reflects, "Almost immediately, the book gave me a right to sit at the table—a right to play, if you will. It moved me into a brand new space, the empathy and technology conundrum. People wanted to talk to me about this idea; they wanted me to be a thought partner with them. Basically, the book expanded my portfolio and gave me more areas to serve clients and make money while being fully intellectually engaged."

6

Push:
A Guide to Living an All Out Life:
The Story of Orangetheory Fitness
by Ellen Latham

In 2010, Orangetheory Fitness (OTF) pioneered a new fitness concept—interval group personal training. Five years later, founder Ellen Latham published a book chronicling her entrepreneurial journey. The book gave her readers a transparent view of her company, the principles behind it, and the passion it took to construct one of the fastest growing fitness brands in the world.

Ellen explains that her goal in writing *Push: A Guide to Living an All Out Life: The Story of Orangetheory Fitness* was to supplement her clients' connections with their OTF studios and to engage more people in a workout she knows works. The goal was to help people push past fear inside and outside the studio.

She comments, "We've found that the same thought process that pushes you through a challenging workout is also how you work through difficult life situations. That's why, through the book, we wanted to communicate the history of the workout, how OTF came to be, and the fundamental pillars of our dynamic studio and brand."

A coupon for two free workouts inside the book encouraged readers to give OTF a try. The response has been incredible.

Ellen gets a lot of energy from public speaking. She used her industry connections to create buzz that helped to market the book as well as OTF.

She explains, "When I speak, I go deeper into detail so audiences feel they are getting a special scoop on the brand and the OTF story. The book helped cement the relationship and became a guide for fitness and life."

Who knew how important it could be to get comfortable being uncomfortable?

Although their topics, audiences, and goals are diverse, these six books share several core elements:

1. A helpful, not self-serving, approach

2. A provocative title and book cover design

3. An engaging style

It's really that simple. Apply this basic formula to your future book—preferably before you write it.

Chapter **6**

TIPS FOR SUCCESS

Books magnify the "gravitas"
of authors and their brands.

Creating a book that will establish credibility, showcase expertise, and brand you as a desirable business partner isn't rocket science. It just requires you to incorporate some best practices that will ensure the success of your BAMT. With that in mind, enjoy the following recap of tips and lessons we've observed working with highly successful authors crafting high-impact business books.

1. Effective marketing in the twenty-first century helps rather than sells. So too with business books.

2. Books no longer need to be tomes to be successful. Keep it to 120–150 pages, with each chapter readable in 10–15 minutes or less.

3. Business books should be user friendly and add value. They can explore complicated topics, but they need to do so clearly, without mucking things up.

4. "I" is a low-value word and redundant if your name is on the cover. Avoid it and write in the third person.

5. Biz buzz books, or mini business books under a hundred pages with fast-read thoughts and business epiphanies, can be very effective and are quick to produce.

6. Find something you can own to create a word of mouth influenza of interest, i.e., word of book, or WOB. This might mean coining a phrase, branding a process or insight, or offering a fresh road map or process to solve a pervasive or unrecognized problem.

7. People like working with smart people and smart brands. A book signals that you and your company are the right fit for the job.

8. The best business books address a compelling problem and solve it with actionable ideas while looking ahead to what's next.

9. The title, cover, and opening paragraph mean everything.

10. Online content marketing is both easy to ignore and perishable. A thoughtfully constructed business book provides a sustainable respite from the 24–7 grind to replenish digital content.

11. Books move the sales process into the third person, making authors more credible and validating thought leadership and brand claims.

12. The cost of this in-perpetuity investment is usually recouped in sales and mind and market share as well as by expanding services and speaking fees.

---

13. The field of politics, the most heated battlefield for influence, constantly overflows with books. There's a reason for this.

14. No one really cares about your personal journey unless you and/or your brand are already famous, as in Mother Teresa or Jeff Bezos famous. You might include personal content with the goal of using yourself as an example of a trend or phenomenon, but that's as far as it goes.

15. Remove self-promoting material so that your book becomes something more than a company brochure. Promote yourself in person or as an adjunct to your book.

16. Be helpful. What do you know that can help your target audience? What can you see that can help solve a problem?

17. Content is king. You gain credibility if your book has useful, sustainable, fresh content.

18. If you think about the strategic use of your book up front, the arrangement of your content and chapters will flow more readily and be more helpful to readers.

19. Design and produce your book as a marketing tool. In many areas, book sales should be seen as a secondary goal.

20. Don't fear hyperbole to get your readers' attention, but overall, be factual and honest and add value with innovative thinking.

21. An altruistic business book proves that you and your brand own the knowledge on a subject and can be relied on as a competent advisor and source.

Epilogue

NO TIME LIKE THE PRESENT

There's no time like the present to write your own BAMT. In light of the incomparable benefits and opportunities, why *wouldn't* you supercharge your brand by writing a game-changing business book for use as a marketing tool?

Don't be daunted. Thousands of others have landed on the moon before you. Writing such a book isn't too expensive, it doesn't take too much time, and any help you need is readily available. The fact is, this invaluable tool for growing market share regardless of your size, target audience, or environment will invigorate both your business and your life.

Appendix A

HIGHLIGHTED BOOKS

Brand Be Nimble: How Big Brands Can Thrive by Acting Like Start-ups by Hunter Thurman

Communication Land Mines! 18 Communication Catastrophes and How to Avoid Them by Marty Clarke

Defend Your Wealth: Protecting Your Assets in an Increasingly Volatile World by Dan Prisciotta

How to Win Friends and Influence People: The Only Book You Need to Lead You to Success by Dale Carnegie

Leadership Rigor: Breakthrough Performance and Productivity Leading Yourself, Teams, and Organizations by Erica Peitler

Open Up and Say Aaah!: Discover...Who You Are Now, Shape...Who You Are Becoming, and Create...What You Want to Experience by Erica Peitler

Purple Cow: Transform Your Business by Being Remarkable by Seth Godin

Push—A Guide to Living an All Out Life: The Story of Orangetheory Fitness by Ellen Latham

Rise Above: How One Man's Search for Mobility Helped the World Get Moving by Ralph Braun

Secrets of the Young & Successful: How to Get Everything You Want Without Waiting a Lifetime by Jennifer Kushell and Scott Kaufman

The Antidote: How to Transform Your Business for the Extreme Challenges of the 21st Century by Anand Sharma and Gary Hourselt

The Empathic Enterprise: Winning by Staying Human in a Digital Age by Marc Brown

The Endangered Customer: Eight Steps to Guarantee Repeat Business by Richard Shapiro

The Four-Hour Workweek: Escape 9–5, Live Anywhere, and Join the New Rich by Timothy Ferriss

The Innovator's Dilemma: When New Technologies Cause Great Firms to Fail by Clayton M. Christensen

The New Business Normal: The Peril and Promise of New Global Priorities by Michael W. Wright

The Not So Big House series by Sarah Susanka

The Perfect Engine: Driving Manufacturing Breakthroughs with the Global Production System by Anand Sharma and Patricia E. Moody

The Power of the Other: The Startling Effect Other People Have on You, from the Boardroom to the Bedroom and Beyond—and What to Do about It by Dr. Henry Cloud

The Sumo Advantage: Leveraging Business Development to Team with Heavyweights and Grow in Any Economy by Bernie Brenner

The Wine Region of Rioja by Ana Fabiano

The World Is Flat: A Brief History of the Twenty-First Century by Thomas L. Friedman

Unleash Your Inner Company: Use Passion and Perseverance to Build Your Ideal Business by John Chisholm

Who Moved My Cheese?: An Amazing Way to Deal with Change in Your Work and in Your Life by Spencer Johnson and Kenneth Blanchard

Whether to Wed: A Legal and Tax Guide for Gay and Lesbian Couples by Scott E. Squillace Esq.

Youtility: Why Smart Marketing Is about Help Not Hype by Jay Baer

Appendix B

SAMPLE TIMELINE TO MARKET YOUR BOOK

A. Two months before launch

- Prepare media list
- Prepare influencer list
- Aggregate and prioritize professional list
- Prepare galley copies
- Send galleys to endorsers and possible foreword candidates; follow up
- Create cover
- Create author bio, author photo
- Create synopsis for overall promotion
- Consider additional printed or digital book summary for marketing purposes

- Convert leading chapter to article and work to place with influential press to acquire press clippings

B. One month before launch

- Write press release and pitch letter
- Draft note from author to A-list clients, prospects, and friends
- Draft promotional copy/description for Amazon
- Seek influencer media reviews with cover and chapter outline
- Establish social media presence for title/subject
- Pitch speaking engagements and corporate visits
- Update personal and brand collateral, "author of"
- Produce mini-video for website showcasing cover (optional)
- Update brand/personal website with book info (add book page)
- Plan launch date
- Investigate launch release via PR newswire, if appropriate
- Plan launch event if key stakeholders are local
- Enlist colleagues and employees to promote launch and availability

C. Launch

- Send release e-mail to list, announce via social media (LinkedIn and Facebook)

- Local, trade, regional pitching
- Update website; add "Buy" button
- Post reviews, press clips, influencer reactions
- Offer team briefings with clients and prospect companies with free books
- Send book to program chairs of relevant association/industry events seeking speakers (particularly regional events and conferences)
- Send book with personal note to VIP list
- Build interactive community on LinkedIn around subject
- Ask clients, "friendlies" to post reviews on Amazon.com and other social media
- Announce in alumni magazine and hometown paper and radio
- Send as holiday and birthday gift
- If business book, offer visit and lecture at MBA schools

About the Authors

MIKE GREECE

Mike is a widely recognized coach and PR Sherpa for business book authors. For more than two decades, his transformative work with business-to-business and business-to-consumer clients has ranged from guiding strategic architecture and content to promoting and leveraging books as marketing tools. Widely acclaimed for his counsel by numerous senior business executives–turned–authors, Mike holds an MA in mass communications from Denver University and a BS from the USAF Academy and is an adjunct professor at NYU's Graduate School of Professional Studies. He has guided successful global PR and integrated marketing programs for an array of companies, including Merck (Coppertone), Western Union, General Electric, Yankelovich Partners, Starter Sportswear, Met Life, the Gary Sinise Foundation, and Reed Elsevier.

JERROLD R. JENKINS

Jerrold is the founder and CEO of Jenkins Group, a premier custom book publishing agency, in Traverse City, Michigan. Since 1988, Jenkins Group has provided premium-quality books for authors, corporations, consultants, and experts with custom solutions that accommodate a variety of budgets and time lines. Jenkins Group also conducts six international book award competitions and provides an array of marketing services for publishers worldwide. Jerrold holds a BS in economics from Alma College. This is his fourth book.

REBECCA CHOWN

Rebecca is an editor and writer based on the Old Mission Peninsula just north of Traverse City, Michigan. Widely recognized for her ability to transform promising ideas into polished writing, she enjoys bringing clarity to confusion and illuminating the ideas that compel authors to write. She has a master's degree from Northern Illinois University and has worked with writers of all backgrounds and interests for nearly three decades.